A Spiritual Bible Story Book For Children

Naeomi

and

Nixon

The things I want them to know
about GOD and His Son Jesus Christ

Linda Eaton-Hall Fulcher

To order additional copies of this book, contact:
Xlibris
844-714-8691
www.Xlibris.com
Orders@Xlibris.com

ISBN: Softcover   978-1-6698-1286-9
        EBook   978-1-6698-1285-2

Library of Congress Control Number: 2022903404

Print information available on the last page

Rev. date: 04/08/2022

Contents

Contents

DEDICATION

This book is dedicated to my four grandchildren, Naeomi Jade, Nixon Joel, Collon, and Malia; and to my three children, Tomiko, Joel, and my son Terrell, whom I lost to cancer in 2005; and to my husband Tom. I love you all and thanks for standing by me.

As for my son Terrell, we miss you so much and wish you were here with us. R.I.P, my son. I will see you again one day in heaven. You are truly missed.

~Mom

This book is written especially for my two youngest grandchildren, Naeomi and Nixon. I love you.

Written, created, illustrated by Linda Eaton Hall- Fulcher

CHAPTER I

ABOUT THE BIBLE

Hey, Naeomi and Nixon, do you know anything about the *Holy Bible*? The Bible tells us about God and how he created the world by just speaking the four words, "Let there be light," and there was light.

In the beginning, God created heaven and the earth. The earth was without form and void, and darkness was upon the face of the earth. And God called the light and darkness on the earth *day and night*, and the evening and morning was the *first day* he created. God said let there be firmament in the midst of the water, and let it divide the waters that were under the firmament from the waters that were above the firmament, and it was so. So God called the firmament *heaven*, so the evening and the morning were the second day.

God said let the water under the heavens be gathered together into one place, and let the dry land appear, and it was so. God called the dry land earth and the gathering together of the waters sea. God saw it was good. And he said, "Let the earth bring forth grass, the herbs that yield seed, and fruit trees that yield fruits according to its kind, whose seed is in itself, on the earth." So the evening and the morning were the *third day*.

God said let there be light in the firmament of the earth for signs and seasons and for days and years, and it was so. God made two great lights, the greater light to rule the day and the lesser light to rule the night. He made the stars and other heavenly bodies too. He set them in heaven to give light to the earth and to rule over the day and the night, and he divided the light from the darkness. God saw it was good, and the evening and morning were the *fourth day*.

God said, "Let the waters abound with an abundance of living creatures, and let birds fly above the earth from across the face of the firmament of heaven, so God created great sea creatures, and every living thing in the sea, and the birds of the air according to their kinds. God saw it was good, and he blessed them, saying, "Be fruitful and multiply, and fill the waters in the sea, and let the birds multiply on the earth. And the evening and morning were the *fifth day*.

God said, "Let the earth bring forth living creatures according to its kind," and it was so. And God made the beast of the earth and every living creature that creeps upon the surface of the earth. God saw it was good, and he said, "Let us make man in our own image." In his image, he created man (us), males and females. Then God blessed us, saying, "Be fruitful and multiply. Go into the earth, and subdue it. Have dominion over the fishes of the sea, the birds of the air, and everything that moves on the earth." And God saw it was good, and the evening and morning were the *sixth day*. And on the *seventh day*, he rested. So you see, Naeomi and Nixon and children of the world, in the Bible, God created it all. He is an awesome God, and he lives in us. So you have to trust him and always do right because he cares for you. Amen!

CHAPTER II

ABOUT GOD

Who is God? Naeomi and Nixon, God is the one who created the heavens and earth. He created you and me. God is love. He created all people of the earth, all animals on the earth, and all things on the earth. God created the whole world in just six days. On the sixth day, he created man and woman, and on the seventh day, he rested from all his works when he saw it was good.

Naeomi and Nixon, did you know that God is someone you can go to when you need help, in times of trouble, or when you are hurt or sick? You can also go (pray) to God to bless your mom, dad, siblings, friends, yourself, and in fact, everybody. You can go to God for their healing too, and he will listen to you and answer your prayers. God won't always come to you when you want him to, but he is always on time when you need him to be there.

God loves all the children of the world and all people of the world. God wants you to love your neighbor as you love yourself and as you want people to love you, so always treat all people right, no matter their color, nationality, or creed, because God is the maker of (them) us all, so we are all God's children and heir to God's throne.

Also, Naeomi and Nixon, God wants you to help others in need. For example, if you meet anyone in need of food, water, clothes, or anything else, and they ask you to help them, you are supposed to give them whatever you can, but that is if you have it to give. Naomi and Nixon, be good to your parents and listen to them. Also, be good to your grandparents because parents and grandparents love their children and grandchildren so much. God wants all of us to do things that are good in his eyes and not to sin (doing bad things). God can see us and hear us, and he records everything we do here on earth. This is because He made us and knew us before we were created in our parent's tummy. He knows about every string of hair on our heads. God knows who we are born to, and he also knows our parents, even before we did. God is our everything. He doesn't want us to go through this life alone. He wants us to call on him for everything, no matter what it is. Just know that God loves us and will forgive us for any bad thing we do, but also know that there are negative consequences for those bad things. Naeomi and Nixon, always fight your battles on your knees, and you will win every time. Love God, love yourself, and love others. Amen!

CHAPTER III

ADAM AND EVE IN THE GARDEN OF EDEN

God planted a garden eastward in Eden, and there he put the man whom he formed, and out of the ground, the Lord God made every tree that is pleasant to the sight and good for food to grow. The tree of life was also in the midst of the garden. It was the tree of knowledge of good and evil. There was also a river that went out of Eden to water the garden, and from there, it parted and formed four river heads.The names of the four river heads were Pishon, Gihon, Hiddekel, and Euphrates. God put Adam in the garden to tend and keep it. God commanded him, saying, "Of every tree of the garden, you may freely eat, but of the tree of knowledge, good and evil, you shall not eat or touch it, for on that day that you shall eat of it, you shall die.

God saw that it was not good for man to be alone, so he decided to make him a helper that was a lot like him. While Adam was asleep, God formed a woman from his ribs and out of the dust of the ground, then breathed into his nostrils to give life. When he was done, he closed up the wound and called the woman Eve. When Adam woke up, God asked him to give all the animals he created names, that whatever he called them would be their names. Some of the names he gave them are monkey, bear, lion, elephant, snake, giraffe, birds, and so on. Adam said to the woman, "You are now the bones of my bones and flesh of my flesh, so she shall be called woman because she was taken out of man."

One day, Eve went into the garden to eat, and suddenly, she saw a snake (satan). The snake told her to eat from the tree of knowledge of good and evil, that she won't die, so she ate of it. Eve went to Adam and asked him to eat the forbidden fruit, telling him that she had eaten of it and didn't die, and he did eat.

Don't be disobedient to God because it comes with consequences. Naeomi and Nixon, always obey God so you won't face bad consequences. He will fight your battles.

CHAPTER IV

NOAH'S ARK

Naeomi and Nixon, do you know what Noah's ark was all about? Well, God said to Noah that he was disappointed in the way the people were doing things on the earth. The people were sinning. He told Noah that he was going to destroy the earth with everyone and everything in it. Noah tried to tell the people about what was going to happen, but no one listened.

God told Noah that he was going to destroy the world with water, that it was going to rain for forty days and forty nights, until everything on the earth was gone. God said to Noah, "I want you to build a big boat (ark) so you can put your family and two of every kind of animal on earth in the boat." Noah was a man who loved the Lord, and the Lord loved him. Noah did not question the Lord on what he asked him to do. God promised Noah that he was never going to destroy the earth like that again.

He made a covenant (agreement) with Noah that there was never going to be a rain or flood that will destroy the earth like that again. He sealed it with a rainbow.

Noah's ark was a massive ship, built at God's command, that saved Noah's family and representatives of every kind of land-dependent, air-breathing animals, from the global flood that took place over 4,300 years ago. The ark was 510 feet long, 85 feet wide, and 51 feet high. It housed several thousand animals God brought to Noah.

CHAPTER V

ABOUT JESUS CHRIST

Naeomi and Nixon and the children of the world, Jesus was the son of the Almighty God. God gave his only begotten son up on the cross to die for our sins. He died and paid the price for all our sins so that we didn't have to do it ourselves. We didn't deserve the things that Jesus did for us. He did it because he loved us, more than we love ourselves.

Jesus wrote his autobiography. Before he was born, John talked about it in the book of John. John was one of Jesus's disciples who followed Jesus on his journey on earth.

God created Jesus in his own image. That means he was made in the image of God and looks like God. The only way you can get to God is to go through his son Jesus Christ. Whatever prayer you have to make, you have to take it to Jesus, and he will take it to the Father for you. But to be able to take your prayers to Jesus, you have to become a believer first. To become a believer, you have to ask God to come into your life and be your Lord and Savior and forgive you for all your sins. Then you will have to repent from all your bad doings, turn all your bad behavior around, and do right in the eyes of God.

Jesus loves children and all people. Jesus is the light of the world. We must always obey him. Jesus walked on the earth as God. The Lord, Jesus Christ, and the Holy Spirit are one person. They are referred to as the Father, the Son, and the Holy Spirit, which is also called the trinity.

Children, the Bible has sixty-six books, starting with the book of Genesis and ending with the book of Revelations. When you want to read your Bible, you can start with the book of Genesis or John, or you can even start from anywhere you feel like starting from. *Just start reading it!* It is always good to read your Bible because it will tell you so much about God and Jesus and how they love and care for us so much. Just trust in him. Amen!

CHAPTER VI

THE NAMES OF JESUS'S TWELVE DISCIPLES

Children, there are twelve disciples (apostles) of Jesus Christ. They are the twelve followers of Christ. They were ordinary men who followed Christ, and they also were very flawed like we are, but Jesus Christ still chose to use them. Their names were

1. Peter
2. James (the son of Zebedee)
3. John (James's brother)
4. Andrew (Peter's brother)
5. Philip
6. Bartholomew
7. Mathew (the tax collector)
8. Thomas
9. James (the son of Alphaeus)
10. Thaddaeus or Judas (the son of James and Lebbaeus)
11. Simon (known as Peter of Canaanite)
12. Judas (betrayer of Jesus)

These are the apostles who followed Jesus in his journey through the world. They were very important to Jesus. As you read your Bible, you will see how important they were.

CHAPTER VII

THE NAMES THEY CALL GOD IN THE BIBLE

1. JEHOVAH - The Lord Our Provider (Genesis 22:14)

2. JEHOVAH NISSI - The Lord Our Banner (Exodus 17:15)

3. SHALOM - The Lord Our Peace (Judges 6:24)

4. JEHOVAH RAAH - The Lord Our Shepherd (Psalms 23:1)

5. TSIDKNES - The Lord Our Righteousness (Jeremiah 23:6)

6. JEHOVAH SHAMMATH - The Lord Is Here, ABBA FATHER - Fo`r you have not receive a spirit of slavery leading to fear again, but you have receive a spirit of adoption as sons by which we cry out "ABBA FATHER" (Ezekiel 48:35)

7. EL-SHADDAI - God Almighty (Genesis 17:1)

These are the names of our God, our Father, by which we call him in our Bible. So, children, remember these names, and there are more names you will learn about our Father. Amen!

CHAPTER VIII

WHAT IS PRAYER?

Naeomi and Nixon and the children of the world, do you know about prayer? Prayer is the practice of the presence of God. It is the place where pride is abandoned and hope is lifted and supplication is made.

Prayer is the place of admitting our need, of adopting humility, and claiming dependence upon God. Prayer is the needful practice of the Christian. Prayer is the exercise of faith and hope. Prayer is the privilege of touching the heart of the father through the son of God, Jesus, our Lord. The Bible speaks much of prayer, but sometimes, too often, we ignore prayer and seek to accomplish in the strength of our own wills those things that we desire to have or happen.

For those of us who are too often guilty of this, we need to bow down on our knees and ask God that the will of God be done above our own. You know, kids, God is sovereign and loving, and he knows what is best for us and others, even if it doesn't always seem to make the most sense. We so often come to the Lord with good answers for requests for our healing conversions and needs, and yet the answers we hope for often do not come.

You have to wait on the Lord and do not doubt him. He is always right on time and never late, and he is always there for you. Children, I just want you to know that when you are praying to God for whatever your needs are, stand in prayer and wait for his answers. He hears you and wants the best for you. Just know that prayers change things for those who love and wait on the Lord. Just trust God and call on him when you are in trouble because he is there for you. Amen!

CHAPTER IX

WHAT IS FAITH?

Children, faith is the substance of things hoped for and the evidence of things not seen. When you pray or ask God for something, believe in him, even though you cannot see or feel him, because he is always there. He said he will never leave you or forsake you. God lives in your heart and walks with you every day. When you are in prayer and on your knees, put your hands together and ask God for whatever you want.He will give it to you. Sometimes you may have to wait for it to happen. Just keep praying and be faithful in your heart and know that God is God and he will answer your prayers. Children, always have faith in what God can do because he can do all things and make us do all things through Christ that strengthens us. God is a loving God. Love him as much as you can because one day we will see God, and we will have to account for all the things we have done on earth (good or bad). Have faith and trust God. Amen!

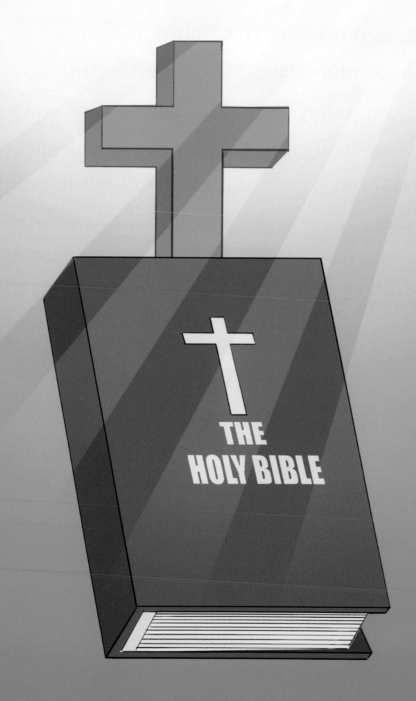

CHAPTER X

SOME OF THE BIBLE'S GREATEST PHRASES

The Lord is omniscient. (He knows all things.)

The Lord is omnipotent. (He is all powerful).

The Lord is omnipresent. (He is always with you.)

The Lord loves you perfectly. He can and will always arrange every circumstance of your life to work out for your good.

Naeomi and Nixon and the children of the world, always trust in God. He will work out all things for your good. Love all people, and I will want all people to love you back.

THE END

Written, created, and illustrated by Linda Eaton Hall-Fulcher Copyright (c) 4/24/2020 lindafulcher061@yahoo.com ladydivamonroe.net

Thank you, everyone for reading this book. I hope every child and every person gets something out of this book. You are all blessed, highly favored, and deeply loved by God and me.

Linda Eaton Hall-Fulcher

Printed in the United States
by Baker & Taylor Publisher Services